for YOU
my ZIGGY FRIEND!

PETS ARE FRIENDS YOU LIKE WHO LIKE YOU RIGHT BACK

ZiGGY

BY Tom Wilson

Sheed Andrews and McMeel, Inc.
Subsidiary of Universal Press Syndicate
Kansas City

GOD MUST HAVE
iNTENDED FOR
eveRYONE TO
HAVE A KiTTeN

...CAUSE He
KEEPS MAKiN
SO MANY OF
THEM !!

Dear Santa,
This may seem like a strange request, but for Christmas could you see your way clear to bring me a box of Kruncho Bisquits, ...a red ball with a bell inside, and a new chew toy

EVERY GOOD DAY BEGINS WITH A LITTLE LOVE !!

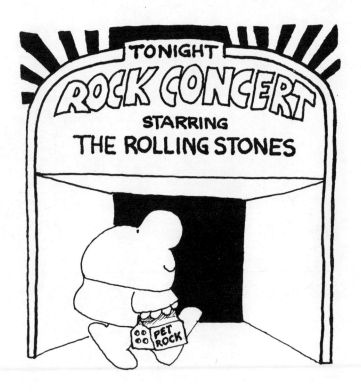

A HUG A DAY
Keeps THE
PSYCHiATRiST AWAY

I'M CONVINCED THAT MUCH OF THE DOG FOOD CONTAINS LARGE AMOUNTS OF CEREAL
...CAUSE HE'LL ONLY EAT IT FOR BREAKFAST!!
FUZZ

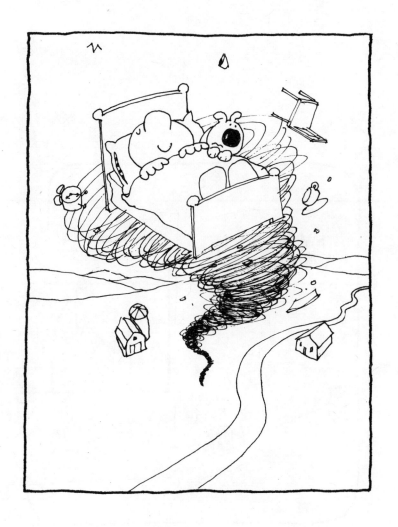

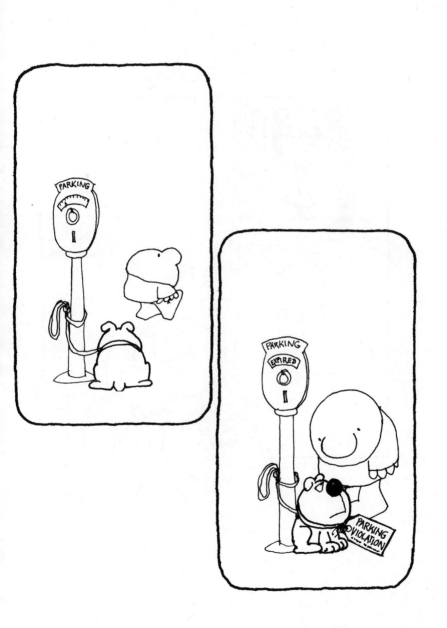

OTHER POPULAR ZIGGY BOOKS:

Never Get Too Personally Involved With Your Own Life
By Tom Wilson
$2.25 (paper)

Promises to Myself: Ziggy's 30 Day Ledger of I Owe Me's
By Tom Wilson
$2.25 (paper)

Life Is Just a Bunch of Ziggys
By Tom Wilson
$1.95 (paper)

Ziggy Coloring Book
By Tom Wilson
$1.50 (paper)

It's a Ziggy World
By Tom Wilson $1.95 (paper)

Plants Are Some of My Favorite People
By Tom Wilson
$1.95 (paper)

Ziggys of the World Unite!
By Tom Wilson
$1.95 (paper)

If you are unable to obtain these books from your local bookseller, they may be ordered from the publisher. Enclose payment with order.

Sheed Andrews and McMeel, Inc.

6700 Squibb Road
Shawnee Mission, Kansas 66202